Their Limiting Beliefs Are Not Yours

The art of distancing yourself when manifesting...

Eleni Sophia – Their Limiting Beliefs are Not Yours

Copyright © 2023 Eleni Sophia – Their Limiting Beliefs are Not Yours

All rights reserved.

ISBN: 978-1-914275-86-9

Perspective Press Global Ltd

Dedicated to you. The most wonderful soul who may be experiencing any sort of hardship.

You may find my words repetitive, but I pray they give you all the reassurance you need.

You were always destined for more; so, ignore their shallow opinions. Use their energy to keep working on yourself.

Keep your focus on self-improvement, and never cease to work on becoming the best version of yourself.

Maintain your steadfast commitment to self-improvement and let the pursuit of becoming the finest version of yourself be your eternal focus.

You've got this.

This is your reminder that their limiting beliefs are not yours; I wrote this book for those of you who are trying to reinvent themselves amidst others' attempts to take you down. The moment you realize how elevated you are and how much purity you radiate, do you really think God wants you on a table like that? Do you genuinely feel God would place a high-value woman like you on a table around people with intentions to take you down? Or those who are waiting for you to do something wrong so they can immediately jump against you? No, he removed you because he knew you didn't deserve to be there. Take this as your sign to work on yourself, to pick up books like this, to understand how precious you are, to understand how Godly you are; he doesn't want you around there. He wants you on a table where you're elevating, he wants you on a table where you're embracing your femininity; where you're unafraid to be yourself, where you're surrounded by opportunities. You'll eventually teach yourself to remove yourself from those who wish to see your downfall. And I understand how much harder it is when this person is inevitably and sadly a part of your life i.e., 'toxic family' but seeing how you can empower yourself through this process is a powerful move. Funny thing is, most often, it's those that have very little going for them or those who don't even have their own life together that want to take down yours. Most of the time there's a threat towards you hence the immediate lash against you - so don't be so disheartened. Your presence probably enrages them, and that's the sad truth; they have so little going for themselves they try and take down the ones who know what they want from this life. This is your reminder that you have everything beautiful in life; you have your mind; you have your hobbies and most importantly you have yourself. You love yourself so endlessly. Please do not allow the presence of small minds to distract you from what really matters. Especially if you have been blessed with someone who would do anything and everything for you. Remember, you deserve all the beautiful things in life. Please, do not allow the presence of small minds to distract you from the visions you have for yourself and your future family. The things that matter the most.

I recently saw a quote that said, 'Sometimes I want to reciprocate people's disrespect but then I look at their lifestyle and how life treats them and that's enough punishment' and I couldn't agree more. Silence is golden - let God deal with it. Keep focused on you angel, you've got this and please don't let their existence distract you from what really matters in life and from the blessings your creator has showered you with. Keep trusting him and he will guide you.

Whatever inspired you to pick up this book, I'm so proud of you. Whether you were in the need of a self-help book or feel drained and you need a place of relativity or someone to understand you, this book is for you. I hope my words soothe like those of a big sister or a mother. I hope you find comfort to return in times of distress and I pray this book is your solace.

I wrote this for those of you who may be going through bullying, for those of you who feel alone and as though you're often misunderstood. Make this book your safe space – a place where you can be truly and authentically yourself without the need for approval of others. A place where you *know* you're good enough, a place where you can call home.

I hope my words help you understand that you are not alone and if there's anyone out there who has made you feel unvalued know that is simply projection. Their opinions hold no importance; what matters most is who you are at your core and how you carry yourself – the opinions *you have of you!*

I want you to know how incredibly wise and strong you are for taking this step. It takes courage to seek understanding, to confront bullying, and to face loneliness. This book is your sanctuary, a place where you can unapologetically be yourself, free from the shackles of others' judgments.

In a world that sometimes feels unforgiving, remember that you are not alone. The hurt, the pain, and the cruelty inflicted upon you are not your burdens to bear. They are the projections of others' insecurities and inadequacies.

These words are here to remind you that you are more than enough just as you are. Greatness lies within you, and this period of hurt you're experiencing is but a passing storm on your journey. It will not define you; it will strengthen you. Remember, 'this too shall pass.' You are destined for remarkable things.

Your story is still being written, and it's a tale of accomplishment, resilience, and unparalleled strength.

The world may not always appreciate your worth, but never forget that you are a gem, and it's their loss if they fail to recognize your brilliance. This book, this message, these words—they are your companions on this journey. They serve as a reminder that you have the power to rise above the pain, to claim your rightful place, and to become the exceptional person you were always meant to be. Embrace your inner strength, for it is the key to unlocking your boundless potential. Your greatness awaits, and nothing can stand in your way.

Make this book is your safe space. It's where you can authentically be yourself, with no need for others' approval. It's a place where you know you're good enough and can call it home. My words are here to remind you that you are not alone, and anyone who has made you feel undervalued is projecting their insecurities. Your opinions of yourself matter the most.

One thing I noticed this year was so many beautiful things were happening but because there was so much in my head, I never remembered what was going on. I needed to stop, pause, and reflect but this wasn't easy; I needed to reprogram myself into understanding how to calm my mind. I needed to write my thoughts to appreciate all that was happening - all that I was missing. All the greatness I was missing because my mind was in chaos. I sat down, in a state of stillness, allowed meditation music to raise my vibration and I felt an endless amount of inspiration surge from within me. That inspiration is right *here,* and I pray you too find a sense of stillness and calm through my words.

Their limiting beliefs are not mine. I have always had everything. All I will ever need comes from my mind. I am blessed. I will always be blessed. I am abundant.

Affirm it.

I am blessed in many ways; there is so much beauty waiting for me. Endless blessings are awaiting my arrival. No matter how chaotic things may seem now, I have hope that my beautiful children will one day protect and love me above all else. They will cherish and adore me, and we will explore the beauties of this world as a loving family. But before that, I must recognize the improvements I need to make in myself to be a great mother, starting with decluttering energies that drain me. Decluttering doesn't just belong in the home; it extends to people too.

Who you surround yourself with is vital in the quality of your life. Imagine growing up with everything, knowing abundance is always there and you begin surrounding yourself with people who have a lack mindset... you've negated all the work your mind has done. I cannot stress this enough – their limiting beliefs are not yours. Just because others have grown up in a certain way it doesn't mean their outlook on life should be the same as yours. And if they try and convince you otherwise, they have overstepped their boundaries and its time you remove yourself to stop allowing them to interfere with your beliefs.

If you wish to have a certain life that may seem bizarre and out of reach for them, continue to believe so, if you wish to have a small home in the countryside with your family, allow yourself to believe so. Just because those around you may think these plans are out of reach, it doesn't mean they are out of reach for you.

You have every right and capability to desire and manifest all that you wish.

A calm heart and a peaceful mind should be at the top of your priority list. Remember, the best is yet to come.

You have lived such a tiny portion of your life - whether you're 16, 25 or 50, there is so much life to live. There is so much to experience. Live. Free yourself from people's opinions, free yourself from limiting beliefs, believe you are capable of anything and everything. Fall in love with your solitude; pray, go to a coffee shop, and allow the warmth from the cup to cover your entire body - be soothe. Be soothe in your own company. Look into space and be grateful that you are here. Allow the rainwater to cleanse you, just *feel*. I want you to feel something again. I want you to feel alive again. Stop letting certain people take from you that you lose sight of how beautiful life is. Because it really is special, I know you used to feel it too. And remember, you deserve it all.

I grew up with everything; we all did. If we're blessed enough to read this book, we grew up with everything. We have food, we have access to clean water, we have warmth. We have everything. We are beyond blessed.

Becoming a person of immense value. Knowing value is within. Everything I will ever need I will find from within.

Once you understand you are the most precious asset you will ever have, you will take yourself places you have never been before; you will unlock the doors to uncharted territories.

Eleni Sophia – Their Limiting Beliefs are Not Yours

My whole life I've had this belief that I will have everything in this world and more - simply because I am deserving. Once you understand the art of manifestation, you'll realize what I'm saying. Recently I've lost sight of who I am and where I'm heading - mostly because of who I am surrounding myself with. I've always been very reserved because I am incredibly protective of my energy and aware of who actually wants the best for me.

I recently found myself expressing thoughts that didn't align with my core beliefs. The power of those you surround yourself with is profound. When you surround yourself with people with limiting beliefs, they inevitably become yours. The way you raise your children, what image you wish to create for yourself or even the life you envision for yourself should be nobody else's business but yours.

Thinking about how things are going to get done is not even an option – they just will. They always have and they always will.

The art of manifesting begins with a single decision to not believe otherwise, you just know these beautiful things are on their way to you. You don't care *how*. They just *will*. That's the secret. Faith.

Contemplating how things will get done is not an option; they simply will. The art of manifesting begins with a single decision to believe unwaveringly that the beautiful things you desire are making their way to you. Have faith. Trust in the process.

Society has brainwashed us into believing in the 'evil eye'. It's brainwashed us to believe if we show off our successes, some random person's negativity is going to stop your blessings. Nobody can destroy or block the blessings your creator has for you. This is such a big myth within brown culture that it holds people back. The whole idea of 'evil eye' is not real. The idea was probably created by some random person and the same ideology has carried itself down for hundreds of years. It's a concept that's been perpetuated for generations. You are in control of what happens to you. Only if you believe in its (nonexistent) power, you'll end up blocking your own blessings. That's why it frustrates me when people say, 'oh you'll get evil eye'. I simply won't allow it. The moment you give that negativity power, you've lost. The sooner you realize society is holding you back and they're creating limiting beliefs for everyone, you've won. Be in control of your own mind; self-awareness is key. Rejuvenate your mind with affirmations and keep educating yourself; always be a student.

There is much more to life than this. You are so much more than this physical body. The entire universe expresses itself through your existence. Allow solutions to flow to you be open to blessings because the moment you understand how deserving you are of all that you desire, you free yourself from external forces that have made you believe otherwise. Their limiting beliefs are not yours.

You are yet to create so many beautiful memories. Beautiful memories are awaiting to be created by you. You are going to have everything you've ever dreamed of. Patience is your best friend and God is your guide. Let Him protect and lead you.

Live in complete certainty, knowing that you will achieve your goals. Each day, take responsibility to move closer to them. Use the space in this book to journal your thoughts. You're at home here.

There must come a point where you cannot allow other's limiting beliefs interfere with yours. Manifesting is a beautiful thing and when you know you're an effortless manifestor, you cannot let others' views interfere yours.

For example, if someone is complaining about money or 'worried' and you are very much aware you have an abundance mindset, money is attracted to you, money finds you beautiful, money cherishes you, if you know you're always going to have money - politely ask them not to project these feelings onto you or politely change the subject. If you're into manifesting anyway, you shouldn't be surrounding yourself with this type of energy anyway. As an effortless manifestor, you are aware abundance if your birthright and you are destined for a wonderful life. If you know you emit money beautifully, please, stop allowing those with limiting beliefs affect your being. Everything is energy - money is energy. The universe sends us these people to test us. When you know you are deserving of all the wonderful and finest things in life, nobody can take that away from you.

Don't let others with contrary views affect your spirit. Energy is everything. When you know you are deserving of life's finest things, no one can take that away from you. And if the finest things in life are a small cottage in the woods with your family – know, you are deserving of the. magnificent things your mind dreams of.

We came forth to this world to have a great time. We came here to do our part to make the world a better place. We came with a purpose to have the best time.

Your dreams and standards of living may seem crazy and out of touch for others but if you know you have every capability within to make these dreams happen, if you are fully aware that your creator will never remove anything that was meant for you, if you know - and when I say know I mean truly, genuinely, at the essence of your soul understand how capable you are, then why must you allow those minds who are not on your vibration to interfere with your goals.

That's one reason why they say to keep your dreams and aspirations to yourself. They tell you to keep your ideas, your plans, your expectations to yourself. Everything is energy and the moment small minds interfere, you lose track.

Just because these dreams might seem unattainable for others it doesn't mean they're unattainable for you. You have a unique purpose and dreams that may seem extraordinary to others, but they're within your reach. Guard your vision against the interference of small minds and stay true to your aspirations.

You know your capabilities and you understand the power of you and your creator – especially when you work together.

Your mind is a magnet. Remember you have the choice whether that is to attract or repel. Seek advice only from those who are where you want to be in life.

The following poems are ones that I had to remind myself of – I lost myself and now I am taking back my power. I will eventually become the woman I have been dreaming about. I just had some inner work to do.

These poems reflect the journey of self-discovery and reclamation. Even when you lose yourself, remember it's all part of the process. Every setback is working in your favour, building you into the powerful person you were meant to be.

I consider myself a high-value woman. I am a soft woman. I am a feminine woman. I am a mother at heart. My heart and mind are strong.

People I meet instantly wish to protect and take care of me because of the way I carry myself. The energy I emit is devoured by many. I know I will always be taken care of.

Being a feminine woman is one of my biggest assets; I understand how to put my foot down, but I also know where to draw the line and be feminine and respectful.

I use the energy people emit to take me down to build on my strengths and to make the world a better place.

I am limitless, I am boundless, I am living my purpose.

I am a high-value woman—soft yet strong, feminine yet resilient. My heart beats with the nurturing spirit of a mother, while my mind stands firm and unyielding. The aura I exude is a magnet for protection and care, and my energy is a feast for those fortunate enough to cross my path.

Being a fully secure woman is one of my biggest assets. I embrace being able to sit at the table alone. I love my own company. I don't need designer bags for validation. I have them for myself. My dreams go beyond the eye of materialism. I have all I'll ever need. My mind is filled with the grace of God. My aura is protected; my creator shields me from anything that brings me no good. I am blessed.

I will make use of all that my creator has given and continues to give me. I have everything I'll ever need. I'll always have everything I'll ever need.

Utilize all that your creator has given you. You have everything you'll ever need. Your creator ensures you lack nothing.

For those who may feel disconnected: with themselves, their creator, or lost sight of their dreams, this is for you. I hope my words help you realign with yourself and help you remember the powerful being you are.

This entire year has been a weird one for me; I found myself crying randomly over things that were so minuscule – sometimes I didn't even know why I was crying. I realised I had lost myself, my relationship with my creator was different and it got to a point where I had to revaluate what was wrong. Sometimes it's best to remove yourself to come back more powerful than before. The main problem was the energy I was surrounding myself with.

This is the girl who absolutely loves herself, who understands what she brings to the table, the girl who knows God loves her and what she is doing for the world. But she lost herself. And she's here to teach you that all these things are okay. Every time something 'goes wrong' it's actually working in your favour. Every time things seem tough; the universe is here building you into the strong woman you were forever meant to be.

And I understand it's okay not to be so strong all the time – surrendering to your creator and asking for help might is the first step. Don't be afraid to ask for help from your creator; he adores you. When you ask, he always hears you.

It is your job to make sure you have the best life. It doesn't matter whether things you're doing haven't been done before. It doesn't matter whether it makes others unhappy. If it makes you happy and you're not bringing harm what is stopping you. Fear? Why must you be so afraid of the opinions of those who don't share the same vision as you. Never take advice from those who are living a life that you don't even desire. Surround yourself with the kind of energy that supports your aspirations.

The best kinds of people will always protect your secrets, no matter how bad things get. They will never hold things against you, and they will protect the friendship you once had.

The types of individuals you need to guard yourself against are those who choose to betray your trust when times get tough. On the other hand, the finest kind of people are the ones who steadfastly protect your secrets, no matter how challenging the circumstances become. They will never use your vulnerabilities against you, and they are determined to safeguard the precious bond of friendship you've built together.

Trust is the golden thread that binds relationships together. Those who respect this sacred bond understand that trust is a steadfast companion, enduring the storms and trials that life may bring. When you encounter individuals who choose to betray your trust, it's a reminder that not everyone is worthy of holding a piece of your heart.

The truest friends, the most honourable souls, recognize that trust is a treasure, one that is built through shared experiences, vulnerability, and a mutual understanding of the importance of protecting each other's secrets.

These cherished individuals understand that no one is perfect, and they won't use your mistakes or vulnerabilities as weapons. Instead, they offer a haven where you can be yourself without fear of judgment or betrayal. They are the keepers of your confidences, the guardians of your trust, and the pillars upon which your friendship is built.

In times of adversity, when the world may seem unkind and unpredictable, the value of such individuals becomes even more apparent. They stand by your side, unwavering, ready to shield your secrets from the storms of life. Their loyalty and integrity shine like beacons in the darkness, reminding you that true friendship is a treasure beyond measure.

So, as you navigate the intricate web of human connections, remember to cherish those who protect your secrets, for they are the ones who honour the essence of trust and the sanctity of true friendship. And in their company, you find not only companionship but also the solace of knowing that you are safe to be yourself, unapologetically and authentically, no matter how challenging life may become.

Your life is so special so stop being so sad about these people who seem to be obsessed and have something to say about your every move and how you choose to live your life. Think about that for a minute, it only takes a miserable person to sit there and try and re-evaluate your life instead of trying to focus and upgrade from their own mistakes.

So, for now sweetheart, focus on healing and upgrading. Stop tolerating this behaviour and stop wondering why they don't like you. Why must you care about their opinions? Why do they matter to you? You are so elevated in life; you are such a powerful woman with endless blessings awaiting her arrival – more than what any of this people can imagine. Stop betraying that little girl in you and start by giving her the love she deserves. You truly deserve to start being kind to yourself again – nobody else's opinions matter. I promise you that.

When you begin to have a higher sense of self-worth, you will not care. And I understand that this is easier said than done but truly understand this, where do you see yourself in 5 years? Realistically, if in this day and age – with everything going on in the world -people are still trying to take from you, you've already won.

Sometimes it's best to remove yourself from limiting mindsets to stop you from losing yourself. I'm sure we've all heard the saying 'you are the 5 people you hang around with' so why must you keep entertaining certain beings?

You should leave a table feeling motivated and encouraged and loved and happy. You shouldn't feel drained and as though someone has sucked the life out of you.

If you wish to be a high-level individual, you must remove yourself from negative mindsets. If you consider yourself a cycle breaker, you must understand their problems are theirs. They stop there. You have every capability within you to stop horrible habits from continuing.

rejuvenate your mind from any energy that wasn't serving you purpose.

No matter what you face the good, the bad and the ugly, it works for you. You will continue to grow from the seeds you plant every day. This book is for you, the one who has been made to feel less than, this book has been crafted for you. I urge you turn your pain to power all of you. Did you really think you could speak so disrespectfully, call me, scream at me and I wasn't going to turn this to my win. News for you, I always win.

You are not for everyone to understand and that's okay.

When you are an outsider, or a high value woman, people want to see your downfall. That's why you must be extra careful with what you say and how you hold yourself because you and I both know if someone else had said the same thing, or if someone else's actions were the same as yours, the situation would be completely overlooked. But because it was *you*, that's why they've made this into such a big deal.

Dealing with those who want to see you fail is not easy - especially if there's some sort of family attachment. But it's so important to understand that 'family' can be toxic too. You must always be upgrading your life - whether it's reading, networking, or working out, use the energy they give you to better yourself. You'll eventually come to a point where you don't even have the energy to react anymore because you are obsessed with improving your life.

Stop giving these people a reaction and stop giving them the satisfaction of trying to bring you down. Remember this, anybody who is genuinely living a happy and successful life is never going to try and take away from your success; it's always the ones who seek to find something to bring you down that are the most miserable.

These people who genuinely have nothing going for themselves are the ones who are waiting for you to mess up so they can immediately jump and scrutinize you. You could be the most angelic, polite, sophisticated, eloquent person but the moment you mess up once, they make you feel like it's the end of the world. Now that's not to say don't take accountability where you have messed up - always be learning and improving your life but never allow anyone to make you feel this way again.

Even if you must cut accessibility to you for a while - Especially if these people do nothing but take from you. If people call you childish for removing yourself to better yourself, then be childish. If protecting your peace is childish then so be it. if self-care means being childish, then embrace your inner child.

But always do what is best for you; give your soul the nourishment it needs. It's about time.

A drunken blessing

One thing about me is I will always turn my pain into power. I will always try to learn from my mistakes and continue to view life as a journey. My mistakes are nobody else's to make me feel bad. My mistakes are here to help me reanalyse my life and to help me see what I need to fix in my life. Most importantly, I know that if I hadn't gotten drunk that evening, certain people's true colours wouldn't have shown, I would be here trying to help and speak kindness to someone who clearly had deep envious thoughts towards me. Someone I trusted but the info I trusted them with, they purposefully kept feelings and emotions hidden so one day they could use them against me until I did something 'wrong' (something they were probably waiting to happen for a very long time.) If I hadn't got drunk, I would be wasting my time on someone who was awaiting my 'downfall.' If I hadn't got drunk, I wouldn't have noticed this person was the biggest serpent around.

So, God, thank you. Thank you for showing me who not to trust, for teaching me to keep my thoughts to myself, for helping me understand I need to protect myself; my goodness, did this drunken blessing teach me the biggest lesson of them all. Thank you for my mind, my perspective, thank you for my endless self-love and most importantly, thank you for tequila.

My own actions taught me to revaluate the things I was doing in my life. Not how others saw me. I then realised; alcohol wasn't the only intoxicating thing I removed from my life – I removed worse.

God will save you from investing time and energy in relationships that are not genuine or healthy, sometimes in the funniest of ways. Sometimes, difficult experiences can serve as a wake-up call and help us prioritize what truly matters in our lives.

And I urge you to try and view life the same way – especially when embarking your self-development journey. Notice how God was protecting you all along.

Protect your peace and reanalyze what you want from life. Everything will flow into place for you.

You will mess up but learning how to forgive yourself is one of the most vital tools you must possess We are our own biggest critics and often people around you will criticize and make you feel small but when you can firmly stand on your ground and understand that you are a high value woman - yes you might have made one mistake - but that doesn't change who you are at your core. When you understand who you truly are you'll never allow people to make you feel this small again. You will mess up but learning how to forgive yourself is one of the most vital tools you must possess.

Do not ever allow small minds to ever make you feel diminished again. Even if you made a mistake and did everything you could to rectify yourself, never allow anyone to speak to you in that way again.

The first step is forgiving yourself. This won't happen overnight. Especially if you feel like you've become this person you never thought you would be. Self-accountability is vital.

Remember that self-forgiveness is a journey, and it's okay to have setbacks along the way. Be patient with yourself and keep working towards becoming the person you want to be. Over time, you can rebuild your self-esteem and learn to like and accept yourself once again.

Start by prioritising you. Often during times of hardship it's best to detach from everything.

You may be trying hard not to lose your mind.
You need to forgive yourself.

The past is in the past. Affirm this, 'with each breath I eradicate any mistakes. I forgive myself.

I free myself from limitations and others' opinions.

I free myself.'

This journey will start when you begin being kind to yourself. You may be feeling lost, don't know who you are anymore. Maybe you don't even feel anything anymore. But you've done a great job by picking this up and I'm proud of you. You should be proud of you.

You may be feeling sad because certain people you were there for once have completely turned on you when you make a mistake.

You might feel as though your time was wasted on these people because they didn't reciprocate the same amount of patience and kindness with you. But it's important to remember that not everyone has the same heart as you. And honestly, living in regret will do nothing but make you feel remorseful and you won't grow from this emotion. Just understand that these people probably needed you at this time and that's okay.

People will see what you have and want to destroy it; they will do everything they can to take what they want away from you because it gives them some sort of weird satisfaction to see others miserable.

They don't understand that only when one truly surrenders and understands the beauty of life, they are truly free.

Remember that your self-worth is not determined by the opinions or actions of others. Continue to see yourself as a high-value woman and focus on your growth, self-care, and the positive relationships in your life. Don't let one incident or negative individuals define your self-perception. You are more than capable of rising above such challenges.

Going from a place of caring for someone once to completely detaching yourself can be hard. Especially if this was a friendship you once valued. But if your soul feels the need to remove itself or if you feel so disrespected you know you must remove yourself, then do it. Take yourself away and learn to find friendships that bring value into your life. You may find that you're the only person in your circle and that doesn't mean that there's anything wrong with you. It just means you respect yourself enough to work on yourself and bring immense value into your life.

Those who try and insert themselves into your business and are so concerned with your relationship and how you live your life have nothing going on in their own. Do you see successful people caring about others' standards of living? Do you see content housewives worrying about how so and so live their lives? No, they are focused on their own priorities, from building their empires to protecting their homes, catering to their men, and raising their children. Only inserting themselves those are the ones who get left behind and have no sense of direction. So, stop becoming upset, stop working yourself up on *why* they care so much; they care so much because life is being hard to them, and they have nothing better to do. Instead, keep focusing on yourself, building, and working on your own priorities.

Now just because people are going through pain, it's no excuse to try and bring someone else down. What is actually painful is going through pain and not choosing to break out of it. If you've spent endless time trying to help and they're not accepting your help, focus on yourself.

If they have issues and they're taking it out on others, they need to take a moment of self-reflection and work on themselves. This is not a reflection of you. Stop giving them the power to believe so.

Detach yourself. Detach yourself from their opinions, their views of you and whether you're liked by them.

Only once you truly surrender and understand that there will be a certain group of people that value you and others not so much, you liberate yourself. Realistically, this specific group that you're so worried about probably don't even share the same mindsets and vision as you. That's not so say one is better than the other but if you're on different vibrations, share different frequencies then why must you care?

It's essential to take this time to reanalyse what you want from this world. Maybe you've forgotten, maybe you're confused, or you've lost sight but take this moment of pain and transform it into one that works for you. Try and understand why you're so worried about certain things.

One thing that works well is speaking to myself as though I would my child. Why must you care and worry whether this group likes you? Why must you be so concerned about their opinions if they're talking about you? Why do you give them the power by showing them you're feeling a certain way?

Imagine your child coming home and saying 'mom, I'm upset about …' *insert whatever is bothering you*. How would you speak to them? What would you say? What clarity would you give them?

The moment you heal your inner child by speaking to it the way you wish; you begin your journey of rectifying and healing. You begin nourishing your soul with words you needed and nobody else can give this to you. You won't actually believe anything until you completely believe yourself and until these words don't come from *you.*

The tone and clarity you wish you had when growing up, you'll notice a gradual change in your outlook of life. And gradually, you'll understand that this group probably isn't the best one for you anyway.

We've all heard the saying 'people ruin beautiful things.' When people see what you have and try and ruin it it's important to cherish it even more. Especially if they haven't had the power to come in the way. Hurt people hurt people and that's the sad reality of life. Often, when people come from a place of hurt, they're not focusing on rejuvenating their minds - it's much easier to try and make someone else feel bad or try and take away from someone who is already so fulfilled right? If you notice someone trying to damage your relationship and you're still together, congrats - you have someone so loyal to you and you know they'll stick by you no matter what. You're unbreakable. If the latter happened, they probably did you a favor; if someone can take something you, had it wasn't really yours to begin with. But now it's important to be reserved, aware of who you speak to; you must be conscious of who you're sharing information with. Protect your energy. Vindictive energy comes from a high-level of insecurity and that's why it's so important to protect yourself. To shield yourself and do what's best for you and your family. Those who cannot control their own lives seem to want to urgently have a say in yours. This comes from a place of emotional insecurity. If peace, self-love, and clarity are your priority, you need to protect your peace.

If someone has tried to ruin what you have, you need to immediately remove yourself. You must take yourself out of this situation and do whatever you can to protect. Especially if this is a toxic family member. You need to put your boundaries in place because unfortunately, family can be toxic too and it takes a certain kind of member to try and jeopardies a relationship with you out of envy.

Often, those who envy you will try and do everything to bring you down - whether it's through their words or their actions and that's why you must be wary of who you surround yourself with. You must be careful with the energy you allow around you and to consume you.

Your downfall is fuel to these people; these negative souls who have nothing better to do than bring others down.

Stop sharing things! Stop sharing your goals and plans with small, minded people. Stop telling people your goals. These people are nobody's friends; my darling, I'm going to put this into perspective for you; when somebody doesn't even like themselves, why are you expecting them to like or be impressed by you and your achievements? Stop sharing certain aspects of your life and trusting people so easily. If you want somebody to talk to, talk to God.

Guard your dreams, protect your aura.

Why confide in those who don't even value themselves? Your path is your own; protect it like the precious gem it is. Trust in yourself, and when you need guidance, confide in your inner strength.

Take back your power by not living in fear. Stop fearing these people. Stop allowing them to overstep your boundaries – whether its family or not, how you raise your children is nobody else's business but yours and your partners.

And it's okay to go your own way. To find your own path to not focus on what others expect or want from you Be you. Be authentically you. Be the unapologetically wonderful woman that you are. You've got this.

You will mess up in life, but you need to stop allowing small minds to make you feel rubbish for one mistake you've made.

If someone is making you feel small for something you have already forgiven yourself for, why are you giving them access to you? Why are you allowing them to bring you down?

The masculine man immediately wishes to take care of her and provide because she brings femininity to the table. By femininity I mean her softness, her awareness that a healthy relationship isn't one where its only him that must make her happy; she has immense value here too; she exceeds the expectations of making her house a home, she adores the domestic values of her home.

That's not to say she doesn't have passions of her own, but she understands the beauty in balancing her priorities with what matters most – family.

She doesn't allow modern society to interfere with her beliefs. She will always cater to him as he will her.

Their creator will keep them protected, always.

Her goddess energy is reciprocated in the blessing's God showers her with. Who you surround yourself with is who you become so surround yourself with goodness.

And so, she began by choosing herself first again - by realising she wouldn't entertain what no longer brought her peace.

When you're a secure woman you'll find it's often hard for those who aren't on your vibration to find happiness in your joy. They find it difficult to see you succeed because they know what they're lacking. A secure woman is one who owns up to her mistakes and doesn't dwell on them; she understands her wrongdoings and is willing to improve; she sees every day as an opportunity for growth and self-development. She devours herself in her mistakes because they allow her to grow and become a better person. She doesn't bring other women down for her own pleasure; that's not who she is. She understands the power of her voice and uses it wisely; she's a goddess at her core. She will never allow others to bring her down; when others try and bring her down, she uses that energy to create, to improve, to heal, to come out stronger. Rather than succumbing to negativity, she channels that energy into creativity, self-improvement, and healing. She emerges from every challenge stronger, more determined, and unshaken in her purpose. This woman is inherently different; she's a woman of God; her perspective is different - she'll always win.

Whilst they were trying to tear her down, she was building herself. She was using their negative energy to fuel herself and make herself better. Everything they projected upon her pushed her to rediscover herself. She finds beauty in all faults.

You are here trying to tear down a woman who adores herself; you are here trying to damage a woman who is so secure in herself no entity, nobody or no situation will ever create barriers between the blessings God has in store for her. You are here trying to tear down another woman's manifestations because you find it so hard to work on your own. Keep trying, she's always protected.

A high value woman is one who knows when to *block* people away.

Learn to be around people who fulfil you - go where you are held accountable for your actions but where you can also leave a table feeling replenished.

Go where you are respected – go where you find fulfilment. Go where you are fulfilled.

She is one of the wisest women, yes, she makes mistakes, but she will always learn. The mistakes she makes are helping her evolve into the wonderful wife, incredible mother she was destined to be.
She will always win.

She's the protector of her home, nothing can interrupt her greatness.

The divine feminine embarks on a journey of self-healing and inner purification. Our innate softness and boundless compassion hold immense power, as the divinity of life springs from within us. When we choose to surround ourselves with positivity and support, success and love flow more readily into our lives. Yet, if we persistently engage with those who leave us feeling downcast, the path to success and love becomes more challenging. It's a testament to our wisdom to recognize the influence of our surroundings, and by nurturing ourselves and our environment, we clear a smoother pathway for success and love to embrace us.

And as inspiration surges from within you I urge you to feel the presence of God again.

Why must you allow other people to rule your world? This is your world my angel, begin taking back your power.

You are not defined by your achievements. Your true essence lies within who you are at your core and how you touch the lives of others. Your capacity for love and gratitude defines your graciousness, your kindness, your softness. Remember, you are not just your accomplishments.

Remember who you are. You are the girl who adores herself the one who is ready to walk away from things not meant for her the one who loves journaling and being present you are the girl who is glowing you and the girl who brings so much to the table. You are a woman of God you radiate love kindness positivity and joy. You are the girl who loves to help young women recognize their power. You are the girl who doesn't care about the opinions of others because you know who you are. You are the girl who does not allow small minds to bring her down. You are the girl who knows if she has herself everything will fall back into place. You are the girl who is doing everything she can to love herself again to find herself again. You are the girl who doesn't care about what others are doing she is focused on her own energy. You are the girl who knows how good she is for man; she values him she brings him up he's unafraid to leave her at meetings alone you are the girl who represents him well. You are the girl who knows she will have everything beautiful that she has ever wanted. You will have a beautiful home with loving children who are so influential in the world. You are the girl who has the most wonderful man and is aware she deserves him a million percent. You are the soft girl the happy girl the lovely girl. You are the girl who is doing everything she can to keep promises to herself no matter who may let her down. You are the girl who has and who will always have the most wonderful things in life because she has herself. You are the girl who is so focused on her home on building the foundations of her home that she doesn't care about the opinions of others and what they think of her. You are the girl who knows she has manifested such a wonderful partner and that the both of you think so differently to the rest of the world and not everyone will understand you and how you raise your children. And that's OK because you know you are different and most likely better than most people anyway. You still have the old school mindset that not many others have. But yours is the life that will be the most beautiful and the one that will last forever and for lifetimes to come. It's the everlasting type. You are the girl who understands these things I have written on surface level but the moment you understand them and fill them at your core again you will be OK you will have found yourself again and you will feel this level of self-love radiate from your aura and you will be OK. Everything will be okay. You will have yourself again. So, begin by apologizing to yourself; understand that the hard work on yourself must start now. You've got this. I know you have.

You are a vessel of divine energy, unconcerned with others' judgments, you remain focused on your own path. You understand your worth and are determined to reclaim your self-love. You are unwavering, concentrating on building the foundation of your life, regardless of outside opinions. You have manifested a beautiful future and a loving family. You cherish your wonderful partner and understand your unique path, rooted in an old-school mindset that guarantees everlasting beauty. You have all you ever wanted, primarily because you have yourself. As you rediscover your core, self-love will shine from your aura, and you will be whole once more.

Sometimes, just being yourself is more than enough. Your dedication deserves acknowledgment from those who truly matter. Cease trying to impress those who wouldn't defend your reputation. Who cares if they don't like you? You are pursuing your goals, becoming a better version of yourself, and nurturing your true priorities. You have your mind, you are working hard towards your goals, you are working on becoming a better version of yourself, you are nurturing your home. You are comforting the things that really matter.

When people try and bring you down for your mistakes even after you've tried to rectify them and do whatever you can to fix them... if you have gone above and beyond to apologise and they're still trying to make you feel bad, *thank them*. Thank them for showing you who not to become. Thank them for showing you how to fix your mistakes. Maybe the mistake you made was from a lack of control of something, maybe them constantly nagging you has allowed you to cherish more time alone, to sit in your stillness and embrace your silence. To acknowledge that there is more power in your silence than your explanations.

But no matter what happens, never give them the power over your individuality. Never stop being the gracious woman that you are. Continue giving. Continue being the divine feminine that you are – even if it makes people angry.

Your inner strength allows you to maintain grace and remain authentic, even when it provokes others. Remember who you are. Reconnect with the inner child who longs for your love. This journey may be lonely, but it's also the path to becoming a stronger, better you

Remember who you are.

A wonderful being with more than infinite potential because she recognizes the power within.

It's okay to lose yourself just promise yourself you won't lose it this time around.

And as you sit in your stillness and recognize the power in your solitude, I pray you understand how capable you are. How whole and complete you are. How wonderful you are. How soft you are. I pray you understand how truly marvelous you are. How you hold the purest of intentions and how everything you do is completed with love. How everything you do makes the world stand in awe of your existence. I pray you understand the power you hold. I pray you never lose sight of how incredible you are. I pray you have it all. Your ability to inspire awe in the world is so powerful. Know the power you possess and never lose sight of your incredible worth. You have all the tools to create a fulfilling life, and God's timing is perfect.

You have everything within to live and create a wonderful life for yourself. You have all the tools to create a beautiful livelihood. You've been patient, you've worked hard now we just wait on God's timing. After all, his timing is the most perfect of them all. Despite what you see around you, know that God's blessings are tailor-made for you. He's got you.

My darling, when you feel like giving up and you hear that voice in your head that says, 'your time is coming please be patient with me'. Believe him. Believe that all the hardship you're going through right now is preparing you for an abundance of freedom, success, and happiness. It might be so hard to hear this right now - especially when you look around and everyone seems to have everything that you've ever wanted but understand that when you have faith in your creator, - there's nothing more nourishing for him than someone who trusts in him - everything he's working for in the background is much bigger than what you've ever dreamed of. You're going to have all that you've ever desired. You're going to have more than what you can dream of. Maybe the hardship you're going through is helping you break generational trauma. You are the chosen one my darling and very soon you will reap the benefits of your patience, faith, and commitment to creating a better future for your offspring. Your ancestors cheer you on with endless love.

Your inner child

Do it for her - take that little girl with you wherever you go. Protect that inner child of yours. Speak to her with kindness and understand that even if you don't like who you are right now, that little girl is in there, patient for your return. Know that you'll find the better version of you as you embark upon this journey of self-discovery. You'll reunite with her, and you will feel like you again.

You might have already lost yourself and found yourself and had your awakening. That's so beautiful but you might have lost yourself again and that is also beautiful. Remember, God chooses his strongest soldiers to face the biggest challenges.

This journey will be a lonely one - this may be the first time you're experiencing such a thing. Such loss. Loss from your old self. But here's a spoiler alert, you will be okay.

Think about this, once you overcome this, you're going to be a better version of you. Whatever you are going through, inevitability you will come out of this stronger.

The thought of doing this again, finding yourself, learning to love yourself again might make your tummy churn but I'm here the entire way. You can come back to this book whenever you wish. You have a friend here.

Now it's time to unleash back your power and take back everything.

A powerful woman understands that others' limiting beliefs are not hers; she understands the power of her mind and how she is a magnet; she's not afraid to be authentically herself - even if it frustrates others. Taking advice from those who are not where she wishes to would be the lead to her downfall. Others' opinions will never bring her down; she has no bad bone in her body; she embodies kindness, love, and softness. The moment she understands these qualities she will become unstoppable.

In her unwavering authenticity, she blazes a trail for others to follow. Her kindness is her greatest strength, and her love is a force that heals and transforms. Her softness is not a weakness but a shield against the harshness of the world, allowing her to navigate life's challenges with grace and resilience.

She knows that her power is not just for her own benefit but a beacon for those who seek their own strength. In lifting others up, she rises to even greater heights. Her journey is not without obstacles, but she faces them with unwavering determination, knowing that every setback is a setup for a comeback.

Remember to do it for your inner child. Take her with you wherever you go. Be kind to her, for she waits patiently for your return. You will reunite with her and feel whole once more. Your journey may be lonely, but you will emerge stronger, no matter the setbacks.

She is a testament to the boundless potential within each of us. Her story inspires, her presence uplifts, and her legacy endures. She is the embodiment of a powerful woman, and her impact on the world is immeasurable.

There must come a point in your life where you take a step back and analyse who is taking from you. Taking back your power is a big sacrifice; the journey is a lonely one but it's one you will come out of a lot stronger. You'll begin manifesting wonderful people who genuinely care about you and want the best from you. You'll begin feeling so refreshed.

Often when you feel a group of people, or a specific person try and bring you down its because they see something in you, they wish they had. only a person who comes from a place of lack will try and take from you.

So, when they see you living such a great life, minding your own business, running your business, in a healthy beautiful relationship, they will do everything in their power to get in the way.

Unfortunately, people like this exist all around the world and it's so important to protect your energy and move away.

You'll eventually reach a point where you don't even want to prove your point anymore.

So, take this moment to step away. Stop caring about what others think of you. Disappear for a while; stop being so accessible and understand if you have you, your faith, and the family you've always desired, you'll have everything you'll ever need.

It will amaze you how quickly you can grow and rebuild when you transform their energy in taking you down for your own fuel for growth.

It will amaze you how quickly you can go from a place of pain to power when you make the decision to use their energy to fuel your journey of self-discovery. The moment you make that one decision, you'll be incredibly progressive in your self-love journey.

You'll eventually reach a stage where you'll notice fulfilment, peace and clarity is all that you desire. You might be at that stage right now trying to comprehend everything, you may be at a place of uncertainty and when you are, feel free to re-read this book. Allow yourself to feel pain but always remember to pick yourself back up. Be kind to yourself and unconditionally, be yourself.

People may try to bring me down, believe me, many are awaiting my downfall but, in my heart, I know I am deserving of all that I have. I have manifested everything into my life, the good, the bad, the lessons and the growth. I've even manifested those who want to bring me down into my life. We attract everything and the moment we take accountability, we become unstoppable.

A truly powerful woman understands that only once she is entirely content with all that she has, only then God will bless her with more. She fully grasps that no matter how much success another person may have, no matter how many blessings God may shower another woman with, no matter how happy she is, it doesn't take away from her own.

They may be wishing harm on me, but I know God has me covered, I know nobody on this earth will ever block or remove the blessings my creator has for me. I am unstoppable. I will always win.

Rediscover and embrace your inner strength, worth, and authenticity. It's a reminder that self-forgiveness and self-compassion are essential for personal growth and fulfillment.

Always use their intentions to take you down to work in your favour.

I write this book during a strange emotional time. A friendship I thought was once everlasting completely did a 360 and tried to damage the most important thing in my life. It's to show you family can be toxic too and it's okay. It's for those who feel like outsiders especially around, those who you shouldn't feel guilty for wanting to remove yourself and protect your aura. I wrote this book to try and help anyone who may be feeling lost, those trying to rectify their mistakes but it's to remind you to protect yourself. I'm at the stage of my life where all I crave is peace, self-love, and protection for my family. The family that comes from me.

The art of reinventing yourself begins with a simple step of deciding you will reinvent your life. People change. But make this change because you see yourself.

One of the funniest things is when they try to take down a high-value woman and expect to win. What exactly did you expect? You thought you could break a woman like her? Did you think sitting on a table and talking nonsense and spreading rumors would take her down? You honestly thought that would make her break down? All you did was hurt yourself; anyone in their right mind knows if you're talking rubbish about someone who's not present odds are you're doing it about them too. She was always going to use your energy to work on herself and come back bigger and better than before. She's not going anywhere she's going to continue thriving; her blessings will be tenfold. Oh, you tried to break her? You tried to get rid of her? You cannot get rid of a woman like her; she's hungry; she adores herself; your bitterness can keep trying to remove her but she's not going anywhere; she thrives off your cruelty. She was destined for greatness, her relationship with God is thriving and it's your actions that helped her do that. Those who tried to break her were actually the ones who helped her.

Her mindset will take her places unimaginable to you. God is her greatest provider; he has never failed her; he's going to continue providing and protecting her name from evil spirits like yours.

She has the entire universe in her mind; you cannot expect to be cruel to a woman like that and for her not to place boundaries there.

You really thought you could take her down, but she had the last laugh. She will always win.

Embrace the graciousness you radiate, and don't be concerned if you become the subject of idle talk. The fact that they gossip instead of discussing growth reveals their values. You are destined for greatness, and your unique journey should not be affected by their opinions.

My beautiful soft amazing girl do not allow anyone to take you from your high. You've earned everything you have. You've worked so hard to become this amazing soft woman that you are, why are you so worried baby girl?

Nobody has put in the work you have.

Let go of any worries about the opinions of others, as you attract amazing opportunities and work toward your entrepreneurial goals. Your vision sets you apart from those who lack ambition. You have a unique life awaiting you. Rise above the opinions of those who don't share your vision.

You are one of the most wonderful women to have ever walked this Earth. Please do not let anyone's opinions take you down. You are a woman of God. You embrace your mistakes and use them to your advantage; you become a better woman out of your mistakes. You take criticism and thrive. You know who you are at your core. The world doesn't deserve women like you. You are so special. Don't you ever forget that baby girl.

You have outgrown them. Every time you see them be your gracious you. Stop giving them the attention they don't deserve. Politely say hello and eat your meal, sip your tea, and say your goodbyes. Show your face if you must but be careful with who you trust.

Protect your energy my angel, you are such a gracious being; one of the most wonderful women to have ever walked this Earth.

God has always taken care of things for you so why must you be so concerned about what's going on right now? He's always going to work things out for you. Just like he always has. Patience is your best friend. Anyone who has ever betrayed you or belittled you, forget about them. Why is their existence bothering you so much. Your creator will take care of them in due course baby girl. Just give it time. He will always have your back and your best interest at heart.

You radiate graciousness wherever you go; why are you so worried if you're the topic of the table? The fact people have the time to sit on a table and talk nonsense instead of discussing growth opportunities should show you enough.

You don't even share the same etiquette as them why would you even wish to be seen on a table like that?

And sweetheart, this is your reminder to stop wasting time on their opinions. It's lonely at the top embrace your faults, learn from your mistakes and become the unstoppable woman you were forever destined to be.

When you're God's favourite nobody else's opinions can bring you down. When you're God's favourite, you live your life with ease. You go about your day feeling protected, nourished, and knowing you're always being taken care of. When you're God's favourite, there's a higher power taking care of her always.

When you know you're God's favourite, why must you care that you're the least favourited by people in that room?

He's given you blessings upon blessings. When you know you're God's favourite, you walk through life with ease; you embrace your faults and simply just rise. Know you're God's favourite, always.

Walk into a room where people don't like you and own it. Cherish every moment. I thrive off that energy.

Look at you sweetheart, you're attracting so many amazing opportunities. You're en route to becoming the best entrepreneur in your field. You're outwitting outrageous behaviour and learning and embracing opportunities. So why must you work yourself up about the opinions of those who are nowhere near your level. Those who don't share the same ambitions or visions.

My darling, you'll eventually reach a stage where you surrender yourself; I urge you to come back here whenever you wish. I know many of my words were repetitive, but I hope I have given you all the reassurance you need.

I have a very different life destined for me. Much more than anyone in this bloodline can even imagine. There are endless blessings awaiting my arrival. I know I will have everything. This standard of living just doesn't sit right with me it never has. You must rise above that. Remember, you're destined for greatness.

You value the importance of surrounding yourself with positive and supportive people who uplift and respect you. Your strength and determination to focus on your own growth and well-being are admirable. You are unapologetically yourself, and you understand that your self-worth is not determined by the opinions or actions of others.

You are a high-value woman who continues to evolve and grow, using challenges and setbacks as opportunities for personal development. You embrace your divine feminine energy and recognize the power it holds in your life.

Your message is a testament to self-empowerment and self-love. Keep embracing your authenticity and cherishing your journey of growth and healing. You have a powerful and inspiring perspective on life.

If you had told me at the beginning of this year, I would be writing something on forgiveness I wouldn't have believed you. I never thought I would be in this position to forgive someone so close to me because I never thought they were capable of hurting me; you know when it's that one person you don't think could ever hurt you and you have such high hopes and expectations and you're left disappointed by their constant let downs, I'm talking about that kind of pain. I recently sat in a state of meditation and heard this voice that said, 'forgiveness will set you free.' That little girl inside of you needs to find peace again, she needs to find comfort in knowing all is well and she can only reach that state of harmony when she forgives. You may be in a stage where you're having to forgive without having received an apology and that's also okay. You need to take this step for yourself. First, understand forgiveness is more about you than them. Forgiveness is far from weakness; the moment you forgive, you begin your own healing journey. You slowly begin releasing all the anger, emotions, distress, and start being more in the moment, you understand that pain was here to help you learn and grow. You'll eventually be more composed, and you'll look forward to going about your life because you've surrendered and set yourself free. You're not the same person you were at the beginning of this year and that's okay. Give yourself this cure; do this for yourself. Once you learn to forgive, an aura of peace will surround you. Forgiveness will enlarge your future; for your own peace of mind forgive. Please do it for that little girl inside of you. You deserve peace.

Copyright © 2023 Eleni Sophia – Their Limiting Beliefs are Not Yours

All rights reserved.

ISBN: 978-1-914275-86-9

Perspective Press Global Ltd

Also, by Eleni Sophia

'This One's for You' a poetry collection about the power of self-love and finding oneself.

'From Ours to Yours' a collection written by Eleni Sophia & pn.writes – where the couple discuss the nonexistent honeymoon phase, interfaith, and the power of appreciation.

'Perspective by Sophia'- a motivational book, where Sophia simplifies the 'law of attraction' and encourages you on living a life that you love, just by changing your mindsets!

'Good Morning to Goodnight' the rawest collection about 'love' and first heartbreak.

'Breaking the Cycle' a collection of the power of breaking generational cycles, embracing your femininity and the beauty in balancing a career and motherhood.

Eleni Sophia – Their Limiting Beliefs are Not Yours

She's the type of woman you know is going to have it all. Just one look at her and you know. Not because other people believe in her, but because she believes in herself. She's the one breaking all the generational curses; she's known as the 'rule breaker and the troublemaker.' And she's okay with that. The outside noise is just noise. We often hear, 'Tradition is nothing but advice from the dead' and my goodness, how true is that?! She's forever the protector of her future home, partner, and children. And as she becomes aligned and in tune with her higher self, she embodies her truth. Clothed in self-love, filled with ambition, and protected. You'll fall in love with her magic. She knows she will have it all.
– Breaking the Cycle by Eleni Sophia

Wish them the very best And let them walk away If they don't want to be a part of your life anymore Maybe it's time for this particular journey to end. And I know it's hard It is so incredibly hard; You're left wondering what you did wrong But I urge you to shift your perspective; If you can give so much compassion to the wrong one Think about how much you will be able to give to the one meant for you. The fact that you were able to show so much emotion shows how much you can love, and that is truly magnificent.
Maybe one day you will cross paths grown and evolved
You will look back with clarity And realize why things happened
If they are meant to be in your life Inevitably, It will happen. For now, Continue to put yourself first It's finally time to start making yourself a priority Putting your happiness first. You deserve everything this world has to offer and more Learn to give it to yourself first
You will see why.
– This One's for You by Eleni Sophia

About the Publisher:

Perspective Press Global is an independent publishing firm representing authors under the age of 20.

At Perspective Press Global, our mission is to inspire young aspiring authors that there is no such thing as being 'too young;' your voices deserve to be heard.

The firm was founded based on Sophia's struggle to find representation when she was a 13-year-old writer.
We now have published young talent from around the globe – including, the UK, Albania, Kosovo, Ireland, and Australia!

If you're interested in joining our team, please visit our submissions page at perspectivepressglobal.com and come say hello over on Instagram @PerspectivePressGlobal

Signed copies of all books can be found on perspectivepressglobal.com

For Eleni Sophia's work follow @EleniiSophia

www.ingramcontent.com/pod-product-compliance
Lightning Source LLC
Chambersburg PA
CBHW030121100526
44591CB00009B/487